THE TOLL

Luke Wright is a poet and broadcaster. His poetry stage shows have toured the world and played sold-out runs in London and Edinburgh. He is a regular contributor to BBC Radio and his verse documentary on Channel 4 was nominated for a Grierson Award. His first collection, *Mondeo Man*, was published in 2013. His first play, *What I Learned from Johnny Bevan*, won a Fringe First Award, The Stage Award For Acting Excellence and The Saboteur Award for Best Spoken Word Show. He lives in Suffolk.

ALSO BY LUKE WRIGHT

POETRY

Mondeo Man (Penned in the Margins, 2013)
The Vile Ascent Of Lucien Gore And What The People Did
   (Nasty Little Press, 2011)
High Performance (Nasty Little Press, 2009)

VERSE DRAMA

What I Learned from Johnny Bevan (Penned in the Margins, 2016)

NON-FICTION

Who Writes This Crap? with Joel Stickley (Penguin, 2007)

The Toll

Luke Wright

Penned in the Margins
LONDON

PUBLISHED BY PENNED IN THE MARGINS
Toynbee Studios, 28 Commercial Street, London E1 6AB
www.pennedinthemargins.co.uk

The right of Luke Wright to be identified as the author of this work has been asserted by him in accordance with Section 77 of the Copyright, Designs and Patent Act 1988.

First published 2017

Printed in the United Kingdom by TJ International

ISBN
978-1-908058-42-3

CONTENTS

'O England Heal My Hackneyed Heart'

ACKNOWLEDGEMENTS

I would like to thank Tom Chivers at Penned in the Margins for his editing prowess and all-round decency.

'A12' was first written for *The Rialto*, and then broadcast as part of BBC Local Poets on National Poetry Day 2016. 'O England Heal My Hackneyed Heart' was written for Rebecca Goss's Heart blog. 'The Slow Days' and 'Hoax' were originally broadcast on BBC Radio 4's Saturday Live. 'VAD Hospital, Saffron Walden, 1915' was commissioned by Essex County Council for Now The Last Poppy Has Fallen. 'The Ballad of Edward Dando' was originally a commission for Homework; the poem became a broadside ballad beautifully illustrated by Katie Utting, who is a constant source of inspiration.

Tim Clare spent ages editing 'The Much Harpingon One-way System' for me, so thanks for that. Joe Dunthorne ripped all the rubbish bits out of *The Toll*. Thanks Joe! Thanks to Clare Pollard for continued edits, support and wisdom.

My love and gratitude to Rosy, Katie, Tom, John, and Old Man Newell. And to my Mum and Dad, for obvious reasons.

Special thanks are due to Molly Naylor for saving my life. And finally to my two boys, Aidan and Sam, who are often a lot wiser than their Dad.

To my gentlemen travelling companions —
Dr Garry, Mr Broad and Dr Clarke

§

O England heal my hackneyed heart.
It's shot with guilt and all those nights.
I've shared it far too often, England;
bled it almost dry for eager eyes;
traded it for other hearts
that turned to gristle in my grasp.
Nothing stirs this heart these days;
the party tricks have left it sick.
England heal my hackneyed heart.

O England heal my hackneyed heart.
Show me clumps of pastille homes on hills,
a couple holding hands in Hayle
and chalk-stone words of love in Dorset fields.
Give me roads the motor clings to,
herons over tidal mud
and skinny kids on wild swims —
that Constable-bucolic thing.
England heal my hackneyed heart.

O England heal my hackneyed heart.
Wash it in the North Sea foam,
wrap it up in honey dawn,
make poultices from April dusk
and chicken soup from sleepy days
until it leaps and bangs its cage;
until it thumps me with its thud
and gives me all the grief it should.
England heal my hackneyed heart.

The Toll

The Slow Days

The slow days down to New Year's Eve arrive.
The sherry fug of Christmas afternoon
is swapped for sodden walks and turkey pie
and wrapping paper turns to ash in grates.

In Falmouth, Fishguard, Fakenham and Frodsham
cabin fever seizes naughty boys.
In Narbeth, Nayland, Normanton and Nantwich
fathers rip the batteries out of toys.

And life plods on like boiled Brussels sprouts.
The papers ration out what news they can:
it's floods or sales or National Archive scraps.
Obituaries march sombre to the front.

In Droitwich, Douglas, Dewsbury and Dawlish
the grown-up single children leave for town.
In Bolton, Bedwas, Basingstoke and Barrhead,
the tinsel round the bannisters slips down.

And so we turn to retail parks and malls,
roam listlessly from shop to shop to shop,
half-dazzled in the vast resplendent halls
then join the traffic slowly shunting home.

In Greenock, Glynneath, Glossop, Goole and Gosport
chocolate tins are cellophane and air.
In Halstead, Harlech, Holyhead and Hexham
Grandad guffs with gusto in his chair.

And minutes fall like needles from the tree
as neighbours call round: *is it bins tonight?*
The last aunties are taken to their trains
till finally the last hurrah pulls up.

In Colchester, Kirkcaldy, Cowes and Croydon
they're counting down, all pints and lily-flesh.
In Potton, Prescot, Portishead and Paignton
they snap the dead year off and start afresh.

A12

England's crude appendix scar,
the Essex/Suffolk artery,
salt-baked, potholed, chocked with cars
across the Orwell, Colne and Lea,
the Roman's great, paved *Inter V*.

From Blackwall mouth to Breydon Water,
worlds away from London noise,
the Orbital's delinquent daughter,
friend to suits in souped-up toys
and woodchip-larynxed *good ol' boys*.

Where Witham trees are linocuts
against an endless swirl of blues,
where rat-faced booners slice you up
and eighteen-wheelers rumble-snooze
en route to Brussels, Bonn or Bruges.

Worst road in Britain, so they say,
a dim-lit strip of late-night truth.
You'll never be a motorway;
your tar tattoos are too uncouth,
ground down for years by tyre and hoof.

But I will have you, ruts and all;
your grey macadam's in my bone.

You take me from the fug and sprawl
to Suffolk's icy brine and foam:
you take me home.

Dad Reins

for Sam

The platform-schlep and keycard-shuffle done,
I'm back home again. And, of course, there's change.
New words and habits, but the biggest one:
you've ditched your pram, you're now in baby reins.
No more for us the quick nip up the shop!
You lunge and circle like a moon-faced dog
as I adjust from back-combed jobbing fop
to paunchy dad. My nightly monologue
of measured, risqué quips switched for a set
of weary nags and grinning faux amazement.
I'll step from stage to stage but won't forget
these sweet staccato wobbles up this pavement.
Roam now, my boy, don't worry, you'll be fine.
I'll be your tether, Sam, because you're mine.

Essex Lion

So there we were, like every year,
just up the road from Clacton Pier,
the summer coughing up its last,
the whiff of burger, clink of glass
at Babs and Brian's caravan
(the children palmed off on their nan),
about to have a Bar-be-que,
perhaps a Chardonnay or two,

then chew the fat and smoke cigars,
talk football, property, and cars
and let the evening ebb away
in creamy, moonlit rev-er-ay.
When Barbara squawked, *Oh Lord, fuck me,*
and all and sundry turned to see
a cat-like beast. *By Christ*, said Brian,
Is that...it is...a fucking LION!

A fucking lion! A fucking lion!
That peaceful Clacton campsite nigh on
went berserk. Atomic warning:
campers diving into awnings,
sausages on grills abandoned,
couples pegging it in tandem.
Yet I stopped and gazed in wonder
at the great beast standing yonder.

Silhouette on low-slung sunset:
worlds away from gobshite pundits,
talent shows and loan repayments,
tabloid headlines, mortgage statements,
school fees, drink dos, work dos, taxes,
forms, lists, vote-slips, emails, faxes.
Often I think we're just prisoners
but that lion was the business.

Stoked up coals inside of me
that I've not felt since '93
then vanished in a kick of dust
and left me in the Essex dusk.
Officer, I swear to you,
I'd only had a can or two.
Ask Babs and Linda, we're not lying:
we fucking saw a fucking lion!

Fucking did, it weren't a dog.
No ghost hound from an Essex bog.
It as good as made a beeline
for us and that thing was feline.
Officer! Ask Steve, ask Gabby.
That was no domestic tabby.
Feeding that thing would get trying —
a *Don Juan* of fucking Iams.

A fucking lion! A fucking lion!
I'll still swear it when I'm dying.

Officer, don't be a benny.
What we saw was MGM-y!
A fucking lion! A fucking lion!
Aslan's nephew, Simba's scion.
A fucking lion, bonefide,
the sort of thing what's got a pride.

A fucking lion! A fucking lion!
A fucking lion! A fucking lion!
I'll make this plain, I'm not insane,
that creature had a massive, cunting mane.

Hoax

for Jeremy Beadle

When it's revealed the memoir's a novel,
the pictures were doctored, the find is a fake,
there are some who feel cheated or foolish and tawdry
and those who still cling with an alchemist's faith.

But for others the hoax is a new kind of magic;
it's make-believe roaming reality's realm,
the carnivalesque on a pale Tuesday morning,
a drift down the river with Puck at the helm.

Perhaps we're just hoping when everything's hopeless,
when life has reduced us to pleading and prayers,
a man will remove his beard and his glasses
then smile, point and whisper. *The camera's up there.*

SPAD

A univocal lipogram in A

At a flash bacchanal
cash fans yak.
Blaggards, brash gas Arabs, scant-clad WAGs
and naff Granada drama stars (as banal as pyjamas)
all blah blah blah class A fast
and stab at warm prawn snacks,
Parma ham and gravlax
as a jazz band taps jazz standards
and sad paps snap all that naff razzmatazz.

And what's that?
Sam Snark — a SPAD.
A Lab SPAD!
A Lab SPAD that charms fat cats and blaggards?
Ach Karl Marx's aghast!

Sam's Alan Maran's bag man
and scandal stalks Alan Maran —
all slapdash laws, dark cabals, back hands,
carnal acts, cash shags, data shams,
Afghan wars and VAT scams.
And as scandal rags lack facts,
Alan Maran stands and stands and stands and stands.

Back at that ball, Sam Snark fast-talks a fat cat.
What! That's Stan McNab,
past gangland grandad,
a bad, bad man.

Ha ha ha — Stan! Nah. Ha ha ha.
Marx — pah — that's crap, Sam raps.
Crap! Crap! Crap!
Alan's mantra: Lab's Plan A was a bad plan.
Hark, Sam's hand clamps Stan's arm.
Hand Alan a bank draft, Stan
and Alan can pass a lax tax act. Yah?
Yamas!
Glass clacks
and Stan and Sam lap Cava.

Alas! Raj Slapp, a scandal rag stalwart, stands at that braggart's
        back
and Sam's chat's as flagrant as an Anthrax attack.
Raj scrawls Sam's tall talk,
taps at Whatsapp:
paragraphs and paragraphs that slam Alan Maran,
warts and all.

Thanks man! Raj slaps Sam's back.
That's a splash!

Ah that's bad!

A sax cha-cha-chas
as Sam stands haggard, ash.

And a scandal rag armada attacks.
Hacks trash Alan Maran. SACK! SACK! SACK!

Alan's grand gaff's all sad ballads.
At Sam's stark flat
Sam hangs slack.

The Ballad of Edward Dando, the Celebrated Gormandiser!

Hurrah! It's me! It's ballad time!
Hang some bloody bunting!
Now shut your eyes, sit back, we're off
to eighteen twenty-something.

The belching Georgian after-party,
age of gout and laudanum;
opulence and dropsy spread
to all that could afford them.

The spit-roast swine, Germanic wines,
Beau Brummel's ice-cold quips,
the clash of Nash's symmetry
with George's wobbly bits.

Frayed pantaloons and powdered cheeks
and boo-sucks to the prigs.
The Tory party ruled but it
was all about the wigs.

And dandies dashed in Hackney cabs
from bar to drinking shop;
a gin-soaked trail of tabs until
their foppish waistcoats popped.

And just as in our stage-school age
the slack-jawed Shaznays dream
of being auto-tuned and airbrushed
into pop's hareem

so young men walked the gas-lit streets
of London's rotten heart
with grand ideas to take their lives
and spin them into art.

And so, our hero: Edward Dando,
apprentice to a hatter
(we don't know what his hats were like
but they, dear friends, don't matter).

For days spent stitching hats for chaps
sent Dando mad with boredom;
the line of dandruff decades stretched out
miserably before him.

A member of the lunar race
that history near forgot.
He might, had he been born later,
lined-up with Marx's lot,

but short on ideology
or union or committee
Dando only had a hunch
that life was sort of shitty.

While some were blessed with tails and titles
others buffed their boots
and pickled, stewed and boiled the scraps
of labour's rotten fruits.

> *O who will pave my grave with jewels?*
> *O who will sing of me?*
> *The hatters, blacksmiths, cooks and fools*
> *all piled up like scree.*

And that, thought Dando, shouldn't, *couldn't,*
be the way for him.
So he resolved to live a life
of shellfish, beer and vim.

Off then to an oyster house
with sawdust on the floor;
a pile of shells around his boots.
Our hero ordered more

— *shuck-gulp-drop, shuck-gulp-drop* —
and all washed down with porter,
the swagger of a Don Juan
with his mitts on someone's daughter.

And when he'd swallowed thirty dozen,
Dando belched and sighed,
performed a dance of pocket pats.
What rotten luck! he lied.

I'm sorry Mr Oysterman,
I'll have to see you clear
another day, all right old boy?
Next time I'm passing here.

And had he been a gentleman
the trader would have bowed
and sent him on his merry way,
contented with this vow.

But swagger isn't breeding and
no sooner out the door,
this whistling, cocksure hatter felt
the rough arm of the law.

They banished our voluptuary
to Brixton for a month,
where Dando's raging hunger gave
the other lags the hump.

They shackled him in solitary
for stealing beef and bread,
where there the old screws pummelled him
and boxed his grisly head.

But when his month of gruel was up,
he found the nearest stall,
devoured his dose of protein
and then coughed up bugger all.

Alas! His choice of Oysterman!
This bloke was like a bull
and left our hero in the gutter,
sore, but very full.

So Dando spent his life like this:
from Oyster house to beating,
from shellfish stall to court then gaol
and all for sake of eating

exactly what he wanted to
exactly when he wanted.
For every bristling oysterman
or judge that he affronted

he gained a hundred new admirers.
DANDO STRIKES AGAIN!
Can nothing sate his appetite
for oysters, ale and pain?

Till 1832 rolled around,
the aged Sailor King
now on the throne, austerity
in place of George's bling.

And Dando like his Royal exemplar
saw his fortunes fade.
One August night in Coldbath Fields,
on prisoner parade,

our man collapsed with cholera.
They carted him inside,
where legend, that forgiving mistress,
claims, before he died

they brought a dozen oysters
to his licey prison bed;
he rubbed his stomach, scoffed the lot
and then he fell back — dead.

They buried him in Clerkenwell
beneath St James's bells;
the balladeers sang songs of him
and paved his grave with shells.

Thunder, Lightning, etc.

My brother and I loved a thunderstorm,
the room illuminating like an X-ray;
the steady counting, then the thunder's bellow.

They say that lightning strikes a mile away
for every second counted, but back then
we reckoned that each second was a street.

Three seconds from the flash to clap was school.
Two seconds and *I reckon that's Miss Powell's.*
Now barely one, *It's probably hit the Spar.*

Our lightning strikes would laser half the town,
take down the dreary landmarks of our youth.
A childhood, if you're lucky, should be this.

Safe enough to bathe for fun in terror,
knowing that your parents are downstairs
immune to any horror you could dream.

But now we're in our thirties, lightning's striking
them. Our parents. At first, it isn't often.
The count between the flash and clap so long

you barely notice; miles, not streets away.
But soon it seems there's sad news every month.
And I'm one downstairs, and I'm afraid.

Port Eliot

for Perry

Eleven times I've made that day-long trip,
each undulation etched into my mind.
We throw parties, the smiling Earl once quipped.
It's what we do. And every year I'd find
the time to slump-slouch, knocked-for-six, half-slayed
at that great, grey viaduct, and send
the Western trains tick-tick-tacking their way
across the ancient tracks towards Land's End.
I grew up on those lantern-glowing pathways,
accompanied by mates, then family,
then confidants who saw me through my heartaches;
garrulous and gin-drunk, true and free.
And now, each cold, rent-short November night,
my mind walks the Lynher in fading light.

VAD Hospital, Saffron Walden, 1915

The ancient oak on Freshwell Street
is jaundiced in the Autumn sun
as Clementina clips her way to work.
A window pane plays mirror
to the mid-blue of her uniform
and though she's late, she stops stock-still and stares.

The red cross on the armband,
the starched white of the hat,
black boots that pinch, the bag balm on her palms.
Pulled in, pinned back, with pale blue eyes,
it takes the girl a breathless beat
to realise it's her who's staring back.

It's Clem. *Our Clem.* The messy-haired
adventurer and story queen,
Pied Piper to her brothers, lost in June.
But no one's called her Clem for months.
Those summers seem an age ago.
They linger like a half-remembered tune.

The chance to go and *do her bit*
had won against her life at home.
She'd kissed her mum and hugged the boys to bits.
But as she pitted guilt against
adventure with the VAD

she never stopped to think what it might do.

And now she knows: this woman here
will never lead a squawking gang
of children through the Essex water fields.
And as the thought occurs to her,
September fills her pale blue eyes;
she blinks and blinks and blinks then turns away.

Watch

for Aidan

Like my dad, my Christmas job, it seems,
is balling wrapping paper into bags.

You tear through plastic junk you'll soon forget
until one more, held back to last: a watch.

We sit together, watching seconds tick.
Wow, Dad, you say. *It's going really fast.*

The Pretender

A univocal lipogram in E

The Pretender's sets were legend:
deft sneers, clever self-refs, even lewd metered verse.

He skewered keen MPs,
sex pest peers, repellent geezers.

Even revered elders engendered the Pretender's cheerless vehemence:
"Revered elders? Meh. Sheltered twerps!" he tweeted.
(Seventy-three retweets.)

The Pretender sent meek depressed men berserk:
"Très clever! Excellent Greeks refs."

He rendered hecklers speechless:
"Eh?"

The Express detested The Pretender:
"END THESE HELL-BENT LEFT-LED EVENTS!"

Elsewhere, esteemed Fleet Streeters penned keen sentences.
"Best. Jester. Ever!"

The Pretenders sets were pressed: LPs, CDs, DVDs.
The Pretender decked the sleeves: svelte, velveteen.

Yet between sets, The Pretender festered.
He kept secrets, tempests, deep deep entrenchments.

Endless, fevered weeks spent clenched:
rejected, bent, spent, sleet drenched, wrenched.

Leeches peddled The Pretender's merch.
Schemers fleeced The Pretender senseless.

Fermented Best Westerns greeted The Pretender wherever he went.
Weed wrecked, he never slept.

He descended. Extreme spleen-phlegm drenched regrets,
bejewelled the Pretender's new sets.

He eschewed genteel speech.
He retched depressed vexes, beer-drenched belches.

The meek men were perplexed:
"These recent weeks The Pretender's less clever. Let's see Stew Lee!"

The Fleet Streeters served lesser references:
"Ex-Best Jester Ever! Even Lenny Henry Better."

The hecklers spewed needle-edged heckles.
The Pretender let them.

Week seven, eleven-week stretch,
heckled he ended the set. Left.

Left the B 'n' B beds. Left the Fleet Streeters.
Left the meek men, schemers, leeches.

Wet-eyed, The Pretender crept the rented streets;
dented, he peeled the pretence.

He remembered the weeks pre the DVDs,
the Best Westerns, pre the endless references.

The Pretender trembled, then knelt,
then went elsewhere.

The Much Harpingon One-way System

Welcome to Much Harpingon, a classic English town:
a butcher, baker, grocer's shop, a church of some renown,
a florist, little tearoom, chemist, countless diddy places
that peddle pricey knick-knacks, a pub chocked full of racists,

an offie where the owner is an expert on his booze,
a Tesco on the outskirts which they loathe, but always use.
There's those who read the *Guardian*, there's those who read the *Sun*,
and those who cannot read at all, all here in Harpingon.

Now zoom in on the high street and the well-kempt junior school
where parents suck fags by the gates (I know right, pretty cool);
where streams of vehicles and their owners honk and sometimes bellow
while threading past the 4x4s parked sqwonk on double yellows.

Where puce-faced cabbies teach the children fancy new expressions
and German truckers share choice vocab seldom heard in lessons;
where tiny tots like drunkards stagger perilously near
to having some great eighteen-wheeler lop off half an ear.

That was until they fired up the bureaucratic pistons:
proposed at one sparse council sesh a brand new one-way system.
All nine of them unanimously voted for a loop
which meant the motors wouldn't mount the kerbs right by the troop

of mothers and their wobbly brats retreating from the bell.

But little did they know they'd just unleashed unbridled hell.
Instead of threading past the kiddies, traffic had to go
a new route past the massive gaffs that lined Clematis Row.

All Georgian windows, scrumptious red brick, front doors flanked by bay,
the type of place that makes a bard go slightly Thomas Gray.
The front lawns lush beneath the shade of rugged elms and yews.
You want me lorry down here, love? − *LIKE HELL WE BLOODY DO!*

And so the Priggs and Crapps and Smyths who called that road their own
soon whipped out pads of Basildon Bond and settled near the phone.
Dixie, darling, have you heard ... I know, I know, it's rotten ...
that ghastly little council man ... this shall not be forgotten.

They launched a pamphlet war that made old Thomas Paine look lazy;
and though the prose was full of oomph, the facts were kind of hazy.
This scheme was dreamed by Eurocrats, it costs three million pounds!
The loss of passing trade will mean the shops will all close down.

And naturally if one keeps shop in some lost rural part,
this kind of thing will give one palpitations of the heart.
And so one Sunday afternoon three hundred locals came
and marched the streets of Harpingon and cried: *NOT IN OUR NAME!*

And Mrs Smyth & Crapp & Prigg (wax jackets, walkie-talkies)
worked the crowd like Tory wives. *The council's telling porkies.*
I know! The swines, we're on your side. Now come on, fall in line.
The megaphone please, Sarah-Jane - LET'S HEAR IT ONE MORE TIME!

Their husbands oiled the press, their patter reasonable and lacquered,
and made sure everybody had a felt-tip-scripted placard
marked FREE OUR TOWN! and other slogans sure to raise the hackles.
(But traffic cones and bollards? Well, they're not exactly shackles.)

And there among the shopkeepers and Smyths and Crapps and Priggs
partaking in this pantomime were parents with their kids.
The folk for whom this system was intended for, for safety,
now faced the local telly crews and then pronounced quite gravely:

That one-ways thing, that's bad, that is, that Mr Smyth he told us —
that means the town will have to close and all them shops what sold us
stuff will not be there and that's a shame that is, it's cos
of Eurocraps in Europe, but we like things like they was.

The knobbly, narked-off faces of Harpovians now haunted
the business ends of local rags, where councillors were taunted
until those beige, well-meaning patsies knew they couldn't win,
until the plans lay shredded in the Council's wheelie bin.

Of course a few of you will think Much Harpingon is brilliant:
Why, in this age of apathy, it's noble and resilient.
So let me put this in perspective, skip a month or three,
and change has reared its head again. The local library

is sadly due for closure — *MORE CUTS!* the rag laments.
That is until some locals mount a spirited defence
to save this cheery info point, this meeting place for clubs,
this web café for pensioners, this vital local hub;

where kids whose parents don't own books can come and read for free,
a breastplate in the armoured suit of class mobility.
For well run libraries are more than novels on the shelf;
they're windows on a warmer life, a different kind of wealth.

And though the locals tried their best, their push was kind of quiet —
a lack of time or contacts or proclivity to riot
and so they wrote to Prigg and co: *Could you a lend hand?*
Another march like yours might make council understand.

And sure enough a letter came back, posted second class:
We know, it's such a tragedy, it's left us all aghast.
If only we could help you, but alack 'the man' has won.
Still, it's not all doom and gloom, there's always Amazon.

One Trick Bishop

Back when he was just a parson,
the local scout hut fell to arson.
So in this dire, desperate hour
he abseiled down his belfry tower.

Cassock flapping, mental hair,
nervous thumbs-up, little prayer.
A vicar doing silly things;
it fondly plucks the ticker's strings.

The Synod press team gave it welly
(got a bit on local telly).
Crazy Cleric! cried *The Sun*
and soon enough near everyone

had heard about the Vicar's stunt
and stumped up for the scout hut fund;
the giant cheques, those wincing smiles
that one associates with piles.

Oh what success! And, though they mocked,
it made up for his dwindling flock.
His spirits, which would weekly dampen,
dried off when he strapped on crampons.

Frankly put, his gauche descent,

it made him feel more relevant.
So, like a nun (excuse this bit),
he made a habit out of it

and carried on once he made Bishop.
General Synod was explicit:
*Headlines, Bishop? Bravo! Least
it's not another PAEDO PRIEST*

eh? Carry on! And so he did.
Each season saw another bid.
On Red Nose Day, on Cancer Week,
the bishop's maladroit technique

would garner quids for worthy causes:
frail cats, dyslexic horses,
wartime widows, battered belles.
The Wugged Weverend of Wappels

(as Wossy dubbed him) clipped on clips,
dug his heels, got to grips,
posed stiffly for the grim-faced pap
then chatted with the usual hack.

He'd try to get some godly quote in
(every year they left him hoping).
Till later when he read the thing:
Always with the abseiling!

Never once a piece of scripture!
After time the Bish would sit there
with the paper, feeling glum,
as page five showed his dangling bum.

And Mrs Bish would then assert,
I don't know why you bother Bert!
But Bishops like to help the meek
and so he turned a harnessed cheek

and carried on through hail and snow;
and though his flock refused to grow,
the public never tired of him,
stood grinning in his climbing trim.

Famous in the bishopric
for only having the one trick.
For most shirk sermons if they can
but, Christ Alive, there's good in man

and good he saw, yes good and love,
when he descended from above.

The Bastard of Bungay

A crate of Merlot, well demolished;
one part pickled, one part polished;
lost since caning was abolished:
bend over for the Bastard of Bungay.

A tom's been kicked down Earsham Street;
on Castle Lane an ear gets tweaked;
a puppy beats a swift retreat:
trick or trick, it's the bastard of Bungay.

Britain now? Gone to the dogs!
What happened to the Epilogue?
Bagging Area? What's a blog?
Get flogged by the Bastard of Bungay.

A gauche ballet of fumbles and involuntary twitching.
I like my women like I like my coffee ... In the kitchen.

Corner table, gout pout on;
there, man and Harris are at one;
the speed of a slug, the grace of a don:
pom-poms for the Bastard of Bungay

Mental illness? No such thing.
Love? A tussle for a ring.
Elvis Presley? Couldn't sing.

Tring-tring, it's the Bastard of Bungay.

Who lumbers like a sodden cow,
all buckling cane and dripping brow.
Pimp my ride? Oh will you now!
Bow to the Bastard of Bungay.

In early evening dappled light he thought he spied his youth
lost somewhere near the bottom of a bottle of vermouth.

His pocket watch a metronome
by which he lives his days alone.
An app? What that when it's at home?
Groan for the Bastard of Bungay.

Tory party? Lost their way.
Of late it seems the whole world's gay!
An endless march of wretched days
laid out for the Bastard of Bungay.

The hour's late, his eyes are bleary.
Why's the weather always dreary?
Elizabeth ... I miss you dearly.

Can anybody hear me?
Can anybody hear me?

IDS

A univocal lipogram in I
for Iain Duncan Smith

This is IDS.
This swinish thin-grin spilling cringing scripts is IDS.
This priggish birch whip,
this piss-dripping fright-witch
with whitish skin wig,
this jiggling tit hitting skint Brits in mining districts,
this grim Christ victimising sick kids with dwindling titbits.

This is IDS
mimicking kings
ripping ribs in glitz grills
licking his lips thinking *this is bliss*
piling it high, sipping his gin fizz
whilst Brits flinch in windchill
sticking pins in him.

This is IDS
inking his lists: *girls with six kids,*
inciting right-wing print kingpins,
hissing pish, stirring fright
twisting victims till victims stink
till victims swim in ill will
till British dimwits drift right.

This is IDS.
I wish him midnight shifts.
I wish him sinking ships.
I wish him limp dicks.
I wish him shit picnics in drizzling mist (with ISIS).
I wish him blind with hindsight.
I wish him illicit kinship with pigs.

The Toll

Tracy lived on Larner Road,
where fourteen storeys high
she gazed to where Thames industry
met marsh and endless sky,
and dreamed a future of escape —
so brooding, lost and shy.

And mum would have her good days,
all promises and treats —
a trip to KFC for tea,
a DVD, some sweets —
but Tracy learned each victory
brought with it a defeat:

a smashed cup on the kitchen floor,
her dinner in the bin,
the chicken thighs half-thawed and raw
with crispy, charcoal skin;
the gerbil cage a reek of piss,
those days when mum caved in.

She learned to use the microwave
and other tip-toe tasks.
She learned to wash her uniform
and lie when adults asked,
met questions with a question;

she learned to wear a mask.

But most of all she watched the cars
at Dartford's distant toll.
She longed to make those trips herself,
to leave her life of dole,
those hopeless days when everything
seemed out of her control.

Escape into those two dark throats,
to Essex, then beyond,
or high upon the bridge's back
and down into the ponds
and fields of England's 'Garden County' —
break the constant bonds

of youth and passed-down torpor
in a callous, concrete town;
its water stains, graffitied trains,
the shades of grey and brown.
The years accrued like empties,
her barriers came down.

And stayed that way through leaver's day;
a hundred scrawled-on shirts
and giddy talk of sixth form,
but for Tracy it was work,
to pay the toll and drive away
from where the sadness lurked.

Apply, then wait, apply, then wait,
until one afternoon
the morning post brought better news.
She danced around her room:
the Highways Agency wrote back.
Start 21st of June.

So Tracey went to work the toll,
a vast macadam waste,
and on it in her tiny booth
she sat there poker-faced
to take in notes and shell out quids
then watch the cars escape.

As year on year the gales and sunshine
rained down on the booth
and dreary, doleful adulthood
replaced expectant youth,
her hopes became more tangled as
she picked a knotty truth.

Escape, as big and pure as sung
by a schoolgirl in her room
when gin's engulfed her mum again
on a wretched afternoon,
will get drowned out by bills and health
and life's relentless tune.

She saved enough to rent a flat

and make a proper home.
She swapped the old girl's chintzy tat
for modish monochrome.
But as she brushed her teeth that night
it dawned: *Mum's on her own.*

Of course, she'd known that'd be the case
but now she felt a guilt;
she realised, as she looked round
the clean, fresh home she'd built,
that mum had done this, years ago,
before her drunken wilt.

Perhaps it was executives
arguing the toss,
or maybe all the sleazy banter
spewed out by her boss,
but when her rage at Mum had paled
she didn't feel its loss.

Before she'd just been terrified
that she might go that way —
stack sadness on calamity
and just collapse one day.
But now she knew that wasn't her,
she made a plan to stay.

And Tracy went to see her Mum;
she helped her clean and cook.

They shared out pieces of their day
in lieu of children's books;
and every hour they sat and talked
was one less drink she took.

But day on day it did its work —
uneven, sure and slow
until one evening: *Tracy, love
It's just ... Before you go ...*
the words got caught, her dark eyes filled
- *it's all right mum, I know.*

It took another month or so —
a sultry sunburst dawn
so very like the morning
that her daughter had been born.
She groaned then died as Tracy slowly
walked the hospice lawn.

Tracy washed her mother's forehead,
allowed herself some tears
then set about the deathly admin,
paid the rent arrears,
kept a piece or two of tat,
the rest to auctioneers.

And with it most of her stuff too,
until one Saturday,
her notice worked, the moment came.

It had been right to stay;
in doing so she'd earned escape;
paid up, she drove away.

Kelvedon — Liverpool Street

For thirty years the buzzer went at six.
You'd take your breakfast in the lonely half-light;
your milky tea, your marmalade and burnt toast,
the carbon whiff lingering till we rose
to fill the room with Coco Pops and squabbles.
By then, you were at your desk in Bond Street,
out of sight and largely out of mind,
our lives a giddy whirl of girls or Pogs.

Not till I had a summer job at fifteen
did I observe this quiet early ritual:
the briefcase and the brolly (ever cautious),
among the first cars in the station car park
(which I believed gave you a sort of status),
a short walk to the bridge and *Trains to London*.
Perpetually ahead of local bods
who went to work in Colchester or Ipswich.

The fat bloke who sold papers and bad coffee
and greeted tourists with a sigh knew you;
a brisk nod and your *Telegraph* appeared.
You always had the right change, which he liked.
Then on the platform: *Come Luke, we'll wait here.*
The best place for a good seat. You were right.
And I believed, as only children do,
that you, and you alone, had cracked the system.

But coming back at half past five was different;
your straight-backed morning dignity was slouched.
You looked a good deal older then,
as you grabbed fitful scraps of sleep — a slow, sad lean
towards the aisle, until, before you fell,
some well-worn sense would jolt you back upright.
Sometimes you'd snore and I'd shoot eye-balled hatred
at flash young things who raised a sarky brow.

Oh Dad, some days you looked as if you'd walked
those tracks. Although it's only now I know
how heavily fatigue can weigh on us.
The dramas that eclipsed my life that summer
must have felt so flimsy next to yours.
I vowed I'd never work your daily rut.
The trains I catch criss-cross the country's back
but as they do, I lean and fall asleep.

The Back Step

The invoice-chase of Autumn comes
while summer habits linger on.
I chain-smoke on the back step
under worn-out, ten-watt sun.

I know I've got to kick the fags
and get my trainers on again,
clear out this yard of summer junk
and sluice the wheelie bins.

Come Michaelmas the mulchy walks
will win me round to winsome death;
but now I ache for when the wind
had whiskey on her breath.

For fayre and fete and festival;
for when the dead of night was light,
inebriated clarity;
for when the wrongs felt right.

Some days I pass for twenty-five:
I'm ASOS, piss-ups, plans and rage,
a scattergun of quips and puns,
when every drink's a stage.

But other days I feel my age,
when all my cards have been declined,
and sins, like tin cans on a string,
come rattling behind.

Family Funeral

And so, as sure as taxes, they arrive:
these men and women with my father's nose,
last seen mid-childhood at some lunch that dragged.
Now older, mono, crunching up the drive,
arthritic in their unfamiliar clothes:
the funny uncle, the cousin with his fag.

A round of grimaced handshakes then we're in;
where swollen sons stoop down to shrunken mothers
and awkward siblings sit bunched in a line.
We pass the yellowed hymn sheets, it begins.
The cynics fidget with the past, while others
sit waiting for the warm and formal chimes.

Which come, as steady as the carriage clock
which later causes rifts, as a weak-jawed
young celebrant reveals to us a man
we'd known for years. It's not so much a shock,
the things we'd never learned about him, more
a sense that we should talk while we still can.

Outside the light falls, dancing through the leaves;
there's thin-lipped platitudes but no one cries.
A cousin gives his dad a friendly shove,
the children sneak off, and I can't believe
it's taken me so long to realise:
it's not the death that makes us sad, it's love.

Sue's Fourteener

She still says things like *lovely spread* and *wear your Sunday best*,
a glass-near-brimming kind of girl, she'll tell you she's been blessed;

tell anyone that wants to listen - *this estate's all right*,
that drug and violence rumours can be chalked to local spite.

She's always got a sweetie or a smile. Her clothes are bright.
This world's more good than bad, she tells her plump cat every night.

Her little flat is modest: gas fire with ersatz flames,
the sleepy scent of tea and polish, tidy picture frames

that tell a tale that peaked when men wore trousers wide as trees;
a lifetime told in wedding portraits, christenings and *CHEESE!*

Let's join her now, she's here then there, perched primly on settees,
her neat and pushy patter pricked with tidy sips of tea.

She's roping in the neighbours to help her run the fete;
and any chance afforded her, she talks up the estate.

She's sung this song for decades now, and every year there's fewer
stages for her polished act. Friends die and, well, the newer

people in the tower blocks, they're not so keen to talk.
She tries to stop to chat to them while on her evening walk

but most of them just hurry by, or worse, they curse at her;
that's horrible, but Sue's robust and not the least deterred.

This world's more good than bad, she mutters, thinks about her son.
She tries to call him later, but his mobile isn't on.

And so the weeks of planning pass with afternoons of baking,
painting, sewing, chivvying and gentle delegating.

And plenty for the young 'uns too; she wants the kids to come.
She so loves having them about. She wants to meet the mums.

Till Saturday, mid June, arrives: trestle tables, scones,
face-painting for kiddies, bunting, raffles, prizes, songs.

The sun beats down, the sky's a sea of whispy whites and blue.
She hears the same joke countless times: *You fix the weather, Sue?*

And Pat and Pam and other Sue and Steve and Pete are there,
and Gilly and her son, their kids, and Trevor, Trevor's Clare.

And all of them come up to her and thank her, squeeze her arm;
they bring her cakes and tea all day. Trevor calls her *Marm.*

And Sue sits back and drinks it in, the fete, the tower blocks;
they say this place is rough and drab, its reputation shot.

If only they could see it now, she thinks, and sips her tea.
Yes, this estate's more good than bad, I wish more folk agreed.

Then what she knows already dawns: *There's seven hundred flats
and we invited everyone, there's forty here, if that.*

From balconies the kids peer down with fixed, mistrusting stares.
She beckons to them; they don't move. A television blares.

Their parents drunk or tired; some just scared to integrate.
Sue notices how white the faces at her tiny fete.

Then Trevor's there and Pat and Pam. it's time to pack away,
and everyone is leaving, saying, *What a lovely day.*

And packing up is half the fun. Reordering is sweet;
a row of tied-up bin bags, a final sprightly sweep

and Sue is pleased. No, very pleased. She marches to her flat;
she fills the kettle, runs a bath and feeds her chubby cat.

She tries to ring her son: no luck. *He's probably down the pub...*
A shake, a sigh, a smile and then she climbs into the tub.

Then after bath it's sockets off, glass of water, bed;
the cat jumps up to join her and she idly strokes his head.

Then right before she pulls the switch she sees the kids again
and thinks about the massive gulf between herself and them.

The way they'd all just stared at her, how none had joined the fun...
And how long now, how many months since she had seen her son?

But no, don't dwell, we do our best, and life is often bright.
This world's more good than bad, she says, and switches off the light.

Ron's Knock-off Shop

A univocal lipogram in O

Cool London sloths go North to Bolton.
Oz - proto fop on lots of pot.
Hol - posh kook; long socks, blond flop.

Oh. Bolton's not so droll.
Bolton's not got Rococo blocks.
Bolton's not got dons or profs.
Bolton's got no dotcom showrooms,
no comforts for London cohorts.

No, Bolton's got lots of old workshops,
lots of soot
lots of orthodox lowbrows
who mop floors or drown sorrows.
Poor old Bolton. Soz.

       *

Lo! Bolton's got Ron Ock:
odd-job bod, compost gob.
Ron's old shop flogs knock-off dross:
low cost LOCOG togs,
non-cotton 'Cotton Socks',
row on row of dolls for tots,

old promo photos of Björn Borg,
poo-brown ponchos,
off food, crossbows, Goth porn,
docks for 'oPods'.

Ron's old now.
Ron's got no boss.
Ron's got know-how.
Ron knows how to hold forth,
knows how to shop for top knock-off tosh,
knows how to coff-off no good cops.

Front of shop:
Ron plonks bottom down on worn old stool,
scoffs pork roll,
downs shots of Scotch,
croons old Motown songs,
blows soot, blows snot, blows bottom off.
Ron's dog, Bozo, growls soft growls,
both bollocks lollop.

London sloths stroll from block to block.
Oz spots Ron's old shop.

"Oh cooool shop!" Oz hoots. "Hol look!"
Hol looks: "Oh wow!"
Hol drools on Ron's hotchpotch lot of knock-off rot.
"Oh wow! Oh wow! Oh wow! Oh Oz!
Look! Look! Look! Look! Look! Look! Look!"

London sloths blow lots of dosh
on Ron Ock's cosh of knock-off tosh.
Oh Ron Ock!

"Good, good," Ron scoffs. "Now sod off."
"*Sod off*. Oh, so ... NORTH!" Ho ho ho.
Sloths opt not to sod off.
Sloths opt to stroll off, oh so slow.

Ron LOLs,
rolls sloth's dosh.
"London morons."
Locks shop for long month off.
Roll on tomorrow.

On Revisiting John Betjeman's Grave

Ten years ago we slouched up here to you,
a band of gobby boys against the world,
a cobweb string of paying gigs
to keep us from the dole.

We walked up from the beach across the easy
seventh hole, new beards and cocksure hair,
to try and forge ourselves a link,
then fasten it to yours.

The poem that I wrote claimed some success
in this. But mostly it was mimicry:
a ditty dashed like homework then
a rush down to the sea.

Today I come at you from Pityme
alone, down salty Cornish lanes, their hedges
heaving with the goods of May.
Until I reach the course

and see the sunken church behind the green.
Your grave is just the same; the stone looks fresh.
It seems the decade has been kind
to you, but what of me?

For one, I know you so much better now.

Back then you were the bard of railways,
of chintz and church and teashop trysts
in towns I'd never know.

But now I see the terror, shame and sin,
the longing for the lost. Your knife-twist endings
startle like a newborn's cry
then heap their weight on me.

Sick Children

after Betjeman

Frost is creeping up the lead lights
of this skew-whiff Suffolk town
as scores of dog-tired single parents
mop hot brows and hunker down.

Streetlights flicker round the dormers;
landlords toll the bells for time.
Outside, a souped-up SEAT backfires,
bins are trundled, street cats whine.

Bleak December heavy-breathing,
cloaking tiles in silver dust,
while bedroom lights along the high street
faintly glow through icy crusts.

And behind these frosted windows,
single parents share their sheets
with their pale, pathetic children:
towels and bowls and milk-white cheeks.

Close your eyes, exhausted carers.
Stroke and kiss their precious heads.
All too soon come graduations,
lonely lunches, empty beds.

The Minimum Security Prison of the Mind

The food's so good you think you're free;
the screws call in, swap jokes, drink tea
and you know where they keep the key;
you can walk out anytime
from the minimum security prison of the mind.

Your inner eye roams rural streets;
it falls on copses, fields of wheat;
you douse your dreams in sweet deceits;
you can walk out anytime
from the minimum security prison of the mind.

Just one more fag/pill/burger/shot;
now smash the mirror, gild your lot;
hang tinsel in your cell and cough;
you can walk out anytime
from the minimum security prison of the mind.

To be confined is much maligned;
it's not as if the Guv's unkind.
Those bars are blinds, those bars are blinds,
those bare black bars are bijou blinds.
You can walk out anytime
from the minimum security prison of the mind.

Better the devil that lurks inside

than dead-eyed fortune's black-eyed bride;
it's caution more than fear; besides,
you can walk out anytime
from the minimum security prison of the mind.

The sterile reek of piss and pine;
you whistle as you stand in line;
you love her / love them / this is fine;
you can walk out anytime
from the minimum security prison of the mind.

Take back the years this place has borrowed;
step away from easy sorrow:
Going now ... I'll go tomorrow.
I'll go tomorrow. I'll go tomorrow.
You can walk out anytime
from the minimum security prison of the mind.

David, at 68

The kitchen's still with evening light;
there's not much more to do.
So he and Beatrice drain their tea
while Fi pops to the loo.

Good place this, Bea ... Your mum and I ...
he tries to take her hands.
Thanks Dad. Her smile is buckram brisk,
she pats his arm then stands.

And as she does, the oven door
reveals his own reflection;
instinctively he turns away,
a newly-learned reaction.

Fi's back, and then it's scarves and coats.
Mum, don't forget your phone!
The jokey tuts. *I'll warm her up.*
He gives them time alone.

She's chatty on the journey home
and David's glad of that;
awash with sweet parental pride,
they talk about the flat.

She'll have to get that boiler looked at...

Nice view of the square...
The light is lovely in the kitchen...
Yes, she'll be happy there...

He potters in the middle lane,
congratulations himself;
the paid-off mortgage, pension plan,
the fact they have their health;

that they could help their clever daughter
move in somewhere nice.
He's taken by an urge to gush
but thinks about it twice.

I want to watch this show tonight,
she says, and breaks his thoughts.
It's by the chap who wrote that thing,
the one about the courts.

The judges thing? Oh, that was good.
Yes, let's give that a go.
He pictures his new 4K screen
while outside halting snow

begins to fall and David thinks
that this right here's the stuff,
the times they've worked their whole lives for.
He turns the blowers up

and rests his left hand on her knee.
She smiles and tilts her head,
a gesture that he takes to mean
the three words left unsaid.

Then home with toast and decaf tea
to watch the promised thing;
with cat on lap she gently shifts
and rests her weight on him

and feigns a patient interest when
he shows off his TV.
See, you can pause it, like a tape,
get up and make some tea...

And when it starts it's rather good,
perhaps a little slow,
but that's the way these days, he thinks,
that *Noir* thing's back in vogue.

Then, twenty minutes in, the chap
embarks on an affair.
She tenses and his gut jackknifes —
they shift, she clips her hair.

I'm going to make another tea.
Her word are leaden, grim.
Well, I can pause it... shall I pause it?
Fi stops, her back to him.

No, don't, I'm not enjoying it,
she says, still turned away.
I think I'll get an early night.
It's been a long day.

And David's left there with her words,
the memory of her back,
the blank screen standing facing him
his image framed in black.

Lullaby

In half-heeled homes on terraced streets,
the suburbs sing their psalms:
the charger buzz, the deadlock click,
the shrieking, far-off car alarm.

I'm sorry love, it's nothing much —
a carb and protein fix.
Remember how we used to eat
before the kids knocked us for six?

Then here again: the half-bought couch,
the supermarket wine,
the drip-drip of these Netflix nights,
the whittling of our brittle time.

A soggy packed lunch Friday waits
so keep me from the sack.
I can't admit that this is it,
but she's got meetings back-to-back.

And so, to that familiar song:
Oh, you go up, I won't be long.
The sad refrain to Big Ben's bong.
Yes, you go up, I won't be long.

And now it's *Newsnight, Question Time.*

I tell myself that things are fine
as callow SPADS, unreal like Sims,
all sing their grim familiar hymns.

And this is what we'll leave our kids:
the safety net in pieces,
the wolves well versed in double-baa
with tell-tale bloodstains down their fleeces.

What will I leave? Vented spleen?
Four-lettered verbal litter?
A spray of righteous leftist bile
at people just like me on Twitter?

Young, so young and yet so weary,
thumbs like scatterguns.
Another day of useless ire.
Exhausted, I ignored my sons.

I've never cast a selfish vote
nor backed a winner yet,
but here I sit in up-lit comfort;
am I really that upset?

I sing along to Britain's song;
I pick my place among the throng;
I sing their words so I belong.
You go up, I won't be long.

But look around the towns and shires
at all these gleaming steel-glass spires
and retails parks and malls so dear
and tell me who is thriving here.

Apocalyptic Friday sales
and zero hour contract fails;
off-shore fixes, bedroom tax,
while banks and business tip their hats

to politicians flush with chips
and healthcare firm directorships;
the safe seats and consultancies
that wring out our democracy.

And couples like us, cleaved in two,
with no idea what we can do
but proffer up a dour love
to things that can't empower us

or knock back booze or laugh it off,
make strongholds under covers,
or shelve our reason now and then
to scream, scream at each other.

Hungover in Town, Sunday Morning

The cash machines are out of service,
bled of notes for beer and chips;
the dirty city doorsteps strewn
with chicken wings and pizza crusts.

There has been a battle here.
The soldiers long since carted off
in taxi cabs, drape-dragged by mates
half-howling songs of grotty love
in terraced backstreets, buttons popped,
all bloody-gobbed victorious.

And now they roam the airy mall,
showered, shaved and purposeful.
They're zipped up neat to mask the dogs
that nip and growl inside their skulls.

A poster in a cute font asks:
Can you do a drink-free month?
And most could, if they wanted to,
live without the white light nights,
get by without oblivion.
But what then, huh? Just more of this?

More fist-balled strolls around the shops
or box-sets on the half-bought couch?

Do more, they say; enrich your life.
But drink, you see, is not like life.
It's life stopped dead, a slurred pause.
Do more? No thank you, I want less.

Burt Up Pub

A univocal lipogram in U

Slum suburb:
up pub,
gruff bums guff.
Guv pulls suds.
Subs pump dumb club drums.
thumpthumpthumpthumpthumpthumpthump

Burt, Ku-klux gut thug, skulks: sups Bud,
nums grub, thumbs *Sun*, slurs Kurds, hucks lungs,
grunt/burp/grunt/burp/grunt/burp/

BUZZZ. BUZZZ.
Burt's fuck bud Suz.
Suz! ... Huh ... Huh ... Huh?!
Suz dumps Burt.
Sums up Burt's luck.
                              Slut!

Burt sulks.
Burt hunts bunk-ups.
Ruth struts up.
Yum Yum, Burt purrs.
Urgh! Shut-up Tubs! Yuk!
Ruth's curt burst cuts Burt.

Nun! Burt blurts, hurt.

But Ruth's mum turns up:
Burt subs Ruth's mum rum.
Ruth's mum's flush.
Ruth's mum's drunk,
Ruth's mum's jugs jump.
Drugs, Ruth's mum? Burt slurs.
Ruth's mum rubs gums, gurns.
Ruth's mum's numb.

Up turd hut
Burt thumbs Ruth's mum's fur cup.
Ruth's mum rubs Burt's plums.
Ruth's mum sucks Burt's trunk:
lustful slurps, mucus.
Lush! Burt clucks.

Burt bums Ruth's mum's plump butt full thrust,
cups Ruth's mum's sunburnt bust.
Uh-Uh-Uh-Uhhhhhhhhh.
Burt spurts hummus up Ruth's mum's rump.
Ruth's mum trumps.

But Ruth's mum's fuck bud Kurt turns up -
Gulp! Kurt's buff.
Kurt huffs. Kurt puffs. Kurt Kung fus.
Kurt lugs Ruth's mum: *Fun's up slut!*
Burt hurls punch

but Kurt ducks.
Kurt duffs Burt up.
Kurt runs.
Burt slumps.

Burt's skull burns.
Burt's gut hurts,
Burt hurls chunks.

Fuzz turn up.
Drunk, Burt thumps Fuzz.
Dumb stunt.
Fuzz cuff Burt.

Guv shuts up pub.
Suburb lulls.
Dusk. Hush. Dust.

The Ballad of Carlos Cutting

You know the set-up: stately grounds,
half-clotted mud, pink flags,
ironic garb on gekko girls
and onesie-cladded stags,

falafel, shit and churros stench,
a clutch of sponsored stages;
a grim roulette of status
for rock stars through the ages.

'New Band', 'Other,' 'Main', 'Acoustic' —
fame's sad parabola,
as blokes who tacked your face to walls
now hunch through parks with strollers.

And there, half pissed and maudlin,
while hacking through the mud,
I heard a Proustian riff that felt
like bubbles in my blood

and wiped a decade off the table,
spun me back to school,
when Carlos Cutting's strut
was the epitome of cool.

*

Flanked by pretty whippet boys
he called his band The Hedge Priests.
They sounded like a gin house blade flight:
guttural and edgy.

In Camden-purloined naval coats,
more Fagin's gang than Lost Boys,
a litany of snotty misquotes —
Hemingway to Tolstoy.

And drunken boys at festivals,
post-GCSE June,
had Cutting's riffs stitched on their souls
on golden afternoons.

An alabaster urchin king
above the mosh-pit brawls,
his likeness in acrylic paint
on art department walls;

his heartaches etched on army bags
and Tippexed onto folders,
a generation's melodramas
weighing on his shoulders.

Till Mrs Brown came calling
and her perfume fug would hang
around the self-indulgent tracts
that Carlos Cutting sang;

until the riffs that came so easy
lost their lick and spit;
yes, all that counts for nothing
when your second album's shit.

Your third's left uncompleted,
the circus leaves you there,
just fodder for the red-tops —
a washed-up Baudelaire.

　　　　　*

But snap to now and spindly riffs
were spilling from a tent
and, Christ, they stirred my senses
like a former lover's scent.

Inside, on stage, was Carlos Cutting,
scarlet Fender raised,
beating out the fragile lines
that scored my teenage days.

And for a moment it was magic,
rose-tints turned up to ten,
unshackled from my adult angst.
I was a fan again.

But then I looked around the crowd,
sixty, maybe less:

skulking, giggling groups of five
in witty fancy dress.

And when each song was finished
they barfed a sarky roar
until the burly backstage team
sent Carlos on for more.

Skin hanging from those cheek bones,
a hint of mid-life belly,
an unloved, broken toy
for proto-Sloanes in Hunter wellies.

His deep eyes dead, I never saw
a man look so alone.
I couldn't watch. I turned my back
and schlepped my way back home.

With images of Carlos Cutting
as he was and now;
from strutting god whose fretboard
made the holiest of rows

to bored, embarrassed prisoner
whose crime was growing older,
bluntly recreated in the eyes
of his beholders.

We put him on an oily stage

and gazed at him like art —
this thing of beauty, light of life,
we kept him in our hearts,

our young, naive and hopeful hearts.
We followed him in bliss.
In time our hearts grew wearier;
he came to stand for this.

Swimming with Aidan, aged 4

You struggle more than other kids your age,
can't help yourself: picked scabs, pulled threads, left feet.
The effort overwhelms. Half-drowned in rage,
life throws you angry tears and sodden sheets.
But here you're magic, boy. While others tip-toe,
too scared to dunk their heads or leave their depth,
you swagger: grace, grit, guts, and get-me gusto.
You gulp existence down with each gasped breath.
But when our time is up, the shiver-showers
smash your short-lived victory to shards.
That sock just won't go on. You've lost your powers.
I try to offer words but, boy, it's hard.
Aloud, my wise old lines are arid spin;
and so, a hug to keep the victory in.

Essex Lion (... continued)

So back we went to tents and litter,
Essex Lion jokes on Twitter
keeping half the nation laughing;
French crop lads in work suits passing
funny jpegs, lions with
white socks, gold chains and TOWIE wigs.
Of course they didn't see a lion,
sniggering at me and Brian,

Gabby, Linda, Steve and Babs
from lecture halls to backs of cabs,
comparing us on panel shows
to nut jobs spotting UFOs.
A poet even, that was worse:
he sent me up in laboured verse.
I saw him, what a prancing nob!
A poet! Yeah, like that's a job.

But then we see it, news at noon —
this bird holds up her great Maine Coon.
This, she pips, is *Teddy Bear.*
Ooh, he's a one, gets everywhere.
I reckons they saw him y'know.
And holds her poxy moggy so
we see from head to derierre
a sort of glam rock terrier.

She's convinced, but I ain't buying,
looked fucking nothing like a lion!
Cooing in her mumsy sweater:
this'll make our Christmas letter.
While this hawing Guardianista
does his smirking, knowing piece to
camera, saying: *Silly season!*
Packs his satchel, leaves the region.

And that was that, the world moved on.
The Twitterati stopped their puns,
declared themselves quite satisfied.
They were drunk, or just plain lied.
Now no one much remembers it,
my neighbour (twat!) still gives me shit:
Oi mate, he chortles. *Careful, Deborah
thought she might have seen a zebra!*

Joke's on you Dave, fucking fairy!
Zebras — they ain't even scary!
Not like the fucking lion I saw.
I picture it, I hear it roar.
A fucking lion, I swear it mother.
Lion-O's outdoorsy brother!
A fucking lion: the beast, the bloody
Tin Man's chuffing drinking buddy!

A fucking lion! A fucking lion!
I'll fucking swear it when I'm dying.

How can a thing that makes you feel
be anything but fucking real?

§

When your wardrobe towers like a soldier and spews your coats
        like hate speech
and the ivy at your window brings not fairy tales but newsfeeds;
when sleep slips sleek as cave fish from your heavy, itchy eyelids;
when admin tumbles through the grates
and salad drawers conceal your treats
and every human being you meet's a fucking demagogue,
        then think of me —

two Negronis skyward on my crick-inducing sofa,
with the smell of last month's tenant and my heartstrings up in rollers;
touching bruises that you gave me on a time-elastic night out;
my consciousness as thick as sap,
the day's detritus in my lap,
my future free of finger traps, my irises awash,
awash with you.

We will take these toll road Tuesdays and the Skype holes in the WiFi
and the spectres of the exes who streaked senseless through our
        twenties
and the heartaches left to creep on us 'cause back then we were
        strangers
and carry them down railway tracks,
across canals and viaducts,
and on until the years have stacked, and you will cling to me
and I to you.